DINOSAUR JOKES

Compiled by Pam Rosenberg • Illustrated by Mernie Gallagher-Cole

The Child's World

Published by The Child's World®
1980 Lookout Drive
Mankato, MN 56003-1705
800-599-READ
www.childsworld.com

The Child's World®: Mary Berendes, Publishing Director
Editorial Directions, Inc.: E. Russell Primm, Editorial
Director; Lucia Raatma, Copyeditor and Proofreader;
Jennifer Zeiger and Joshua Gregory, Editorial Assistants
The Design Lab: Design and production

Library of Congress Cataloging-in-Publication Data
Dinosaur jokes / compiled by Pam Rosenberg ;
illustrated by Mernie Gallagher-Cole.
    p. cm.
  ISBN 978-1-60253-516-9 (library bound : alk. paper)
  1. Dinosaurs—Juvenile humor. I. Rosenberg, Pam.
  II. Gallagher-Cole, Mernie. III. Title.
  PN6231.D65D56 2010
  818'.6020803625679—dc22   2010002047

Printed in the United States of America
Mankato, Minnesota
July 2010
F11538

ABOUT THE AUTHOR

Pam Rosenberg is the author of more than 50 books for children. She lives near Chicago, Illinois, with her husband and two children.

ABOUT THE ILLUSTRATOR

Mernie Gallagher-Cole lives in Pennsylvania with her husband and two children. She has illustrated many books for The Child's World®.

TABLE OF CONTENTS

4 What?

9 What Do You Call?

12 What Do You Get?

15 How?

17 Did You Hear?

18 Where?

19 Who?

19 Which?

20 Knock, Knock

21 Why?

22 When?

23 Good Question!

Q: What does a giant Tyrannosaurus eat?
A: Anything it wants to!

Q: What's a dinosaur's curse?
A: A Tyrannosaurus hex.

Q: What did the dinosaur say after he caused a car wreck?
A: "I'm so-saurus!"

Q: What's the best way to talk to a Tyrannosaurus rex?
A: Long distance.

Q: What weighs 800 pounds and sticks to the roof of your mouth?

A: A peanut butter and Stegosaurus sandwich.

. . . .

Q: What family does Maiasaura belong to?

A: None of the families in my neighborhood!

. . . .

Q: What game does a Tyrannosaurus rex like to play with humans?

A: Squash.

. . . .

Q: What vehicle does a Tyrannosaurus rex use to travel from planet to planet?

A: A dino-saucer.

. . . .

Q: What's as big as a dinosaur but weighs nothing?

A: A dinosaur's shadow.

. . . .

Q: What did the dinosaur call her shirt-making business?

A: Try Sarah's Tops.

Q: What happened when the dinosaur took the train home?

A: She had to bring it back.

Q: What did the cat say to the dinosaur?

A: "Meow."

Q: What did the caveman say as he slid down the dinosaur's neck?

A: "So long!"

Q: What should you do if a dinosaur is sleeping in your bed?

A: Sleep somewhere else.

Q: What is a Stegosaurus's favorite playground toy?

A: A dino-see-saw-r.

Q: What happened when the dinosaur walked through a cornfield?

A: He made creamed corn.

D-i-n-o-s-a-u-r

Spelling B.

Q: What has a spiked tail, plates on its back, and 16 wheels?
A: A Stegosaurus on roller skates.

....

Q: What comes after extinction?
A: Y-stinction.

....

Q: What comes after y-stinction?
A: Z-end.

....

Q: What is Tyrannosaurus rex's favorite number?
A: Eight.

Q: What do dinosaurs use for the floors of their homes?

A: Rep-tiles.

Q: What do you need to know to teach a dinosaur tricks?

A: More than the dinosaur.

Q: What is in the middle of dinosaurs?

A: The letter S.

Q: What did the dinosaur say when she saw the volcano erupt?

A: "What a lava-ly day!"

Q: What makes more noise than a dinosaur?

A: Two dinosaurs.

Q: What does a Tyrannosaurus do when he takes you out to lunch?

A: First, he pours salt on your head. Then he gets out his fork . . .

Q: What do you call
a leaky dinosaur?
A: A bronto-porous

Q: What do you call a person brave enough
to stick his right hand into the mouth of
a Velociraptor?
A: Lefty.

Q: What do you call it when a Diplodocus
makes a goal in soccer?
A: A dino-score.

9

Q: What do you call a Stegosaurus that never stops talking?

A: A dino-bore.

Q: What do you call a dinosaur that knows a lot of different words?

A: Thesaurus.

Q: What do you call an Allosaurus that isn't feeling well?

A: An Illosaurus.

Q: What do you call a sleeping dinosaur?

A: Stego-snorus.

Q: What do you call a dinosaur that never gives up?

A: Try-try-tryceratops.

Q: What do you call a dinosaur in a cowboy hat and boots?

A: Tyrannosaurus tex.

Q: What do you call a bodybuilding dinosaur?
A: Tyrannosaurus flex.

Q: What do you call a dinosaur who is elected to Congress?
A: Rep. Tile.

Q: What do you call a fossil that doesn't want to work?
A: Lazy bones.

Q: What do you call a dinosaur that's as tall as a house, with long sharp teeth, and 12 claws on each foot?
A: Sir.

WHAT DO YOU GET?

Q: What do you get if you cross a Triceratops with a kangaroo?

A: Tricera-hops.

Q: What do you get when a dinosaur walks through a strawberry patch?

A: Strawberry jam.

Q: What do you get when two dinosaurs get into a car accident?

A: Tyrannosaurus wrecks.

Q: What do you get when you cross a dinosaur with fireworks?

A: Dino-mite.

....

Q: What do you get when you cross a Stegosaurus with a cow?

A: Milk that's too scary to drink!

....

Q: What do you get when you cross a dinosaur with a parrot?

A: I don't know, but when it asks for a cracker, you'd better give it one!

....

Q: What do you get if you cross a mouse with a Triceratops?

A: Huge holes in the baseboards.

....

Q: What do you get when you cross a dinosaur with a glove?

A: I don't know, but you shouldn't stick your hand in it!

Q: What do you get when you cross a dinosaur with a skunk?

A: A big stinker!

Q: What do you get if you cross a dinosaur with a mole?

A: A very big hole in your garden.

Q: What do you get if you cross a pig with a dinosaur?

A: Jurassic pork.

Q: How do you ask a dinosaur to lunch?

A: Tea, Rex?

HOW?

Q: How do you know if a dinosaur is inside your house?

A: Look to see if its tricycle is parked outside.

Q: How did Iguanadons catch flies?

A: With their baseball mitts.

Q: How do you know if there's a dinosaur under your bed?

A: You need a ladder to climb in.

Q: How else do you know if there's a dinosaur under your bed?

A: You bump your nose on the ceiling.

Q: How do you get down from a dinosaur?

A: You don't. You get down from a goose.

Q: How can you tell if there is a dinosaur in your refrigerator?

A: Look for footprints in the pizza.

Q: How many dinosaurs can fit in an empty box?

A: One. After that, the box isn't empty anymore.

Q: How fast should you run when a dinosaur is chasing you?

A: One step faster than the dinosaur.

Q: How do dinosaurs pay their bills?

A: With Tyrannosaurus checks.

Q: How did the dinosaur feel after it ate a pillow?

A: Down in the mouth.

Q: How do you make a dinosaur float?

A: Put a scoop of ice cream in a glass of root beer and add one dinosaur!

Q: Did you hear about the Tyrannosaurus rex who entertained a lot?

A: He always had friends for lunch.

Q: Did you hear about the man who stopped a charging dinosaur?

A: He took away its credit cards.

17

WHERE?

Q: Where do dinosaurs go on vacation?
A: The dino-shore.

Q: Where do dinosaurs go shopping?
A: The dino-store.

Q: Where was the dinosaur when the sun went down?
A: In the dark.

Q: Who leaves money under the pillows of dinosaurs that lose their teeth?

A: The tooth fairy-dactyl.

Q: Who makes the best prehistoric reptile clothes?

A: A dino-sewer.

Q: Which dinosaur loves to eat pancakes?

A: Tri-syrup-tops.

Q: Which dinosaur likes to take pictures?

A: Camarasaurus.

Q: Which kind of dinosaur complains that her shoes are too small?

A: My-foot-is-saurus.

KNOCK, KNOCK

KNOCK, KNOCK.
Who's there?
Dino.
  Dino who?
Dino, I'm too scared
to open the door!

KNOCK, KNOCK.
  Who's there?
Dinosaur.
  Dinosaur who?
Dinosaur that you didn't invite her to the party.

KNOCK, KNOCK.
  Who's there?
Dozen.
  Dozen who?
Dozen anyone around here know how to spell Pterodactyl?

WHY?

Q: Why did the Archaeopteryx catch the worm?

A: Because it was an early bird.

Q: Why didn't the T. rex skeleton attack the museum visitors?

A: He didn't have the guts.

Q: Why did the dinosaur's car stop?

A: Because of a flat tire-annosaurus.

Q: Why did dinosaurs eat raw meat?

A: Because they didn't know how to cook.

Q: Why did the Tyrannosaurus cross the road?

A: To eat the chicken.

Q: Why didn't the dinosaurs let the Stegosaurus play baseball with them?

A: He was always spiking the other players.

Q: Why did the Tyrannosaurus spend three hours staring at an orange juice container?

A: It said "concentrate."

***

Q: Why did the Apatosaurus devour the factory?

A: Because she was a plant eater.

***

Q: Why was the dinosaur afraid of the ocean?

A: Because there was something fishy about it.

WHEN?

Q: When can three dinosaurs get under an umbrella and not get wet?

A: When it isn't raining.

***

Q: When a dinosaur sneezes, what should you do?

A: Get out of the way.

GOOD QUESTION!

BILLY: Did the dinosaur take a bath?

BETTY: Why, is one missing?

JOHN: I keep seeing Stegosauruses with orange polka dots.

NANCY: Have you seen a doctor yet?

JOHN: No, just Stegosauruses with orange polka dots.

23

JOSH: Do you know how long dinosaurs should be fed?

JENNY: The same way short ones are.

JAKE: I lost my pet dinosaur.

SARAH: Why don't you put an ad in the newspaper?

JAKE: What good would that do? He can't read!

RECEPTIONIST: Doctor, there's an invisible dinosaur in the waiting room.

DOCTOR: Tell him I can't see him!

RYAN: Why did the Velociraptor cross the road?

MAGGIE: He didn't, the chicken did.

RYAN: Then why did the chicken cross the road?

MAGGIE: To get away from the Velociraptor!